High Tops:

A Workbook For Teens

Who Have Been

Sexually Abused

HIGH TOPS:

A WORKBOOK FOR TEENS

WHO HAVE BEEN

SEXUALLY ABUSED

Phyllis Spinal-Robinson, L.C.S.W.

and

Randi Easton Wickham, L.C.S.W.

Jalice Publishers
Notre Dame, Indiana

HIGH TOPS:

A WORKBOOK FOR TEENS WHO HAVE BEEN SEXUALLY ABUSED

Published by Jalice Publishers, P.O. Box 455, Notre Dame, IN 46556

Library of Congress Cataloging-in-Publication Data

Spinal-Robinson, Phyllis and Wickham, Randi Easton.

High Tops: A Workbook for Teens Who Have Been Sexually Abused

1. Sexually abused adolescents. 2. Incest victims. 3. Mental Health-Adolescents

I. Spinal-Robinson, Phyllis. II. Wickham, Randi Easton. III. Title.

1993

ISBN 0-9627375-5-0

Dedication and Acknowledgements

We would like to dedicate *High Tops* to all teens who have been hurt by sexual abuse and who are so very brave and courageous.

We are grateful for the therapists who have believed the teens and are helping them with their healing journey.

We would like to thank the following:

Our husbands,...Stephen, for his enthusiasm, humor, encouragement, and emotional support...Byron, for loving encouragement and technical computer assistance...Our families, who have been cheering us on from the sidelines...Randi's sister, Kelly, for her encouragement, affection, and creativity...Judy Chapperon, an inspiring teacher and mentor for Phyllis...Hasina and Shahana, for their invaluable help with Randi's daughter, Celia, and the household...Randi's niece and nephew, Gabrielle and Eric Easton, for beautiful artwork...Phyllis's niece, Marlee Grabiel, for creative artwork contributions...Michael Hays, our artist friend, who provided invaluable expertise and assistance...Des Plaines Valley Community Center and our colleagues there, where we've received much of our training and the clinical experience that enabled us to create this workbook...Our publishers and editor for their dedicated commitment in the field of sexual abuse and to this project...and most importantly, our clients who have taught us what bravery truly is.

Introduction For Teens

Dear Teens,

This workbook has emerged as an outgrowth of our therapeutic work with teen and adult sexual abuse survivors over the past eight years. We have found that weekly therapy with an experienced therapist can and does assist the healing process.

This workbook was written especially for you. It will help you to understand yourself and your feelings. It will also help you to understand and work through many of the feelings and difficulties you may now face as a result of having been abused. It is very important to remember that you are not alone! Current research studies suggest that 1 out of 3 girls and 1 out of 6 boys are sexually abused before they reach the age of 18. You are definitely not alone!

Abuse is something traumatic that happened to you; it is not who you are. You are the one who defines who you are. It is possible to heal from this experience and to go on with your life. This takes time, and it is important to give yourself the time and compassion you will need to heal from this trauma. The information and exercises in this workbook have been designed based on our experience of what has been most helpful to other teens who are recovering from abuse. We wish you success in your healing journey.

Sincerely,

Phyllis & Randi

Table Of Contents

Checklist

Most teens who have been sexually abused will experience many emotional and physical reactions to the abuse. This is very normal. You are not alone in how you feel. It will probably take a while for you to feel okay and safe again. This checklist will help you to notice the kinds of reactions you might be experiencing. See how many of these items seem to fit for you.

Sometimes teens who have been sexually abused...

1._____Have stomachaches, headaches, or other physical problems.

2._____Have bad dreams or nightmares, or have trouble sleeping.

3._____Imagine that all their friends know what happened.

4._____Imagine that no one will like them if they find out about the abuse.

5._____Believe it's their fault.

6._____Feel confused because they may have liked and trusted the person who molested them.

7._____Were afraid to tell anyone what happened to them.

8._____Were afraid they would be punished or get in trouble if they reported the abuse.

9._____Believe their bodies are ugly or dirty.

10._____Have problems with food, such as not eating or eating too much.

11._____Have difficulty concentrating.

12._____Have problems at school.

13._____Feel like running away.

14._____Use drugs or alcohol to block out feelings and pain.

15._____Get into trouble with the police.

16.____Experience extreme shifts in their moods and emotions.

17.____Try or want to hurt themselves.

18.____Feel like they're going crazy.

19.____Feel confused about their sexuality.

20.____Feel ashamed much of the time.

21.____Have problems with dating relationships.

Check any of the items that seem to fit for you.

Secrets

Almost always, teens who have been sexually abused have been asked to keep the abuse a secret, or they have been threatened with the idea that something awful will happen if they tell anyone, or they believe they must keep the abuse secret. It can be very confusing when you are asked to keep this kind of a secret, especially if the person is someone you trust. It can be most confusing and traumatic if the person is a close friend or relative, such as a boyfriend, babysitter, parent, or other relative. Teens often believe they must protect their family members and maintain loyalty to the family by not telling, even though they are being hurt.

Here are some of the things that teens who have been abused may believe.
Which of these do you believe?

I am to blame for what happened.   *yes*   *no*

I asked for it.   *yes*   *no*

I wanted it to happen.   *yes*   *no*

I should have been able to stop it.   *yes*   *no*

My family will be torn apart if people know.   *yes*   *no*

I was too seductive.   *yes*   *no*

The abuser will go to jail.   *yes*   *no*

Everyone will find out about what happened.   *yes*   *no*

I won't be believed.   *yes*   *no*

I will be punished.   *yes*   *no*

No one will like me.   *yes*   *no*

I will be rejected by my family and friends.   *yes*   *no*

Can you think of any other reasons teens might believe that
they have to keep the abuse a secret?

_____

_____

_____

_____

_____

A lot of times, abusers are really slick or sly, and they trick or fool their victims. They may build the teen's trust over a long period of time by *showing affection, buying gifts, showing special treatment or favors, giving money for favors, telling the person that they are very special or that they are the only one who cares about them.*

Can you think of some other ways a teen might be
tricked by an abuser?

_____

_____

_____

_____

_____

_____

Sometimes families keep secrets about abuse. Members of the family may know about the abuse but don't or won't talk about it. This is usually because they are afraid of what will happen if the secret comes out.

If you haven't told about people who have abused you or if you are still being abused, you may not have been ready or you may have felt there was no one you could tell. Try to find someone you can trust, like your therapist, a teacher, a counselor, a family member, or a friend's parent. Try to talk with them about the abuse. They may be able to help you figure out what to do. It is very important to talk to someone and not keep it inside yourself.

****

As you can see, there are many obstacles to telling. Often teens get down on themselves for not having told sooner.

Don't be hard on yourself. You have been very brave for telling about the abuse. This is one of the most important steps that you have taken towards healing. FREQUENTLY, TELLING IS THE WAY TO STOP THE ABUSE.

****

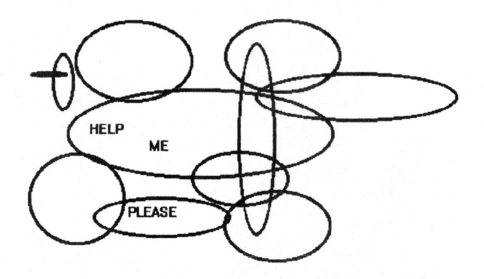

Measuring Scale

This measuring scale will be repeated several times in this workbook so that you can be aware of any changes in your thinking, feeling, or behavior. It will help you to understand more about yourself. You might wish to discuss some of these with your therapist.

Circle one:

I feel scared.	Always	Most of the time	Sometimes	Never
I like myself.	Always	Most of the time	Sometimes	Never
I feel sad.	Always	Most of the time	Sometimes	Never
I'm afraid.	Always	Most of the time	Sometimes	Never
I'm embarrassed.	Always	Most of the time	Sometimes	Never
I feel angry.	Always	Most of the time	Sometimes	Never
I'm happy.	Always	Most of the time	Sometimes	Never
I get upset.	Always	Most of the time	Sometimes	Never
I have nightmares.	Always	Most of the time	Sometimes	Never
I am a good person.	Always	Most of the time	Sometimes	Never
I'm shy.	Always	Most of the time	Sometimes	Never
I have friends.	Always	Most of the time	Sometimes	Never
I like other teens.	Always	Most of the time	Sometimes	Never
My family likes me.	Always	Most of the time	Sometimes	Never
I would be a good friend to have.	Always	Most of the time	Sometimes	Never
I'm excited about growing up.	Always	Most of the time	Sometimes	Never
I like my body.	Always	Most of the time	Sometimes	Never

I worry about how well other teens like me.	Always	Most of the time	Sometimes	Never
I feel attractive.	Always	Most of the time	Sometimes	Never
I feel fat.	Always	Most of the time	Sometimes	Never
I worry about having a boyfriend/girlfriend.	Always	Most of the time	Sometimes	Never
My friends like me.	Always	Most of the time	Sometimes	Never
I feel guilty when I eat.	Always	Most of the time	Sometimes	Never
I'm intelligent.	Always	Most of the time	Sometimes	Never
I'm creative.	Always	Most of the time	Sometimes	Never
I have a good sense of humor.	Always	Most of the time	Sometimes	Never
I am overly sensitive.	Always	Most of the time	Sometimes	Never
I cry.	Always	Most of the time	Sometimes	Never
I am self-conscious.	Always	Most of the time	Sometimes	Never
Other people think highly of me.	Always	Most of the time	Sometimes	Never
I get bored.	Always	Most of the time	Sometimes	Never
I prefer being alone to being with others.	Always	Most of the time	Sometimes	Never
I'm preoccupied with negative thoughts about myself.	Always	Most of the time	Sometimes	Never
I think about hurting myself.	Always	Most of the time	Sometimes	Never
I'd like to have more friends.	Always	Most of the time	Sometimes	Never
Adults care about me.	Always	Most of the time	Sometimes	Never

Feeling Responsible For The Abuse

Often, teens feel ashamed because they believe they are responsible for what happened to them. They may think that they should have been able to fight back or stop the abuse in some way. Abusers are usually physically stronger or may be someone the teen trusts or loves. Abusers frequently seduce teens by giving them special favors, gifts, affection, or attention. Teens may feel as if they must remain loyal to that person. This can be especially confusing for them.

Sometimes, teens believe that it was something about them or something they did that caused the abuse to begin and continue. They often falsely convince themselves that if they change something about themselves or do something differently, the abuse will stop. These beliefs are often reinforced by the abusers who refuse to accept any responsibility and want to deny that they are doing anything wrong. This belief that teens can change or control the situation is a normal reaction to feeling powerless. For example,

Lisa truly believed that if she did better at school and helped take care of her younger brothers, her mother and father would stop fighting and her father would stop molesting her.

Lisa convinced herself that she was in control of the situation, which left her feeling that she was failing and responsible for the abuse.

It may sometimes be difficult to separate things you enjoyed about the relationship with the abuser from the abuse that occurred. It is perfectly normal to miss certain aspects of the relationship, such as feeling special, getting presents or money, being told you are attractive, etc. Abusers are often tricky and use bribes to get what they want. Some teens may feel as if taking a bribe is a good way of getting back at or controlling the abuser. For example,

15 year old Angela would accept money and use of the car from her stepfather, who was molesting her. Over time, she began demanding more and more favors from him. While this would get her what she wanted, she also felt extremely guilty as if she were encouraging the abuse.

Even though Angela took some of her stepfather's bribes, she was not responsible for his actions.

Remember, you are not responsible for the abuser's actions. Adults should never touch kids or teens in sexual ways. NEVER!!!!!!! The abuse did not occur because of something about you or something you did wrong. Changing yourself will not stop the abuse. The abuser must be stopped.

Are there any ways that you feel responsible for the abuse?

_____

_____

_____

_____

Can you think of some things about the relationship that felt good but
left you feeling confused about the abuse?

_____

_____

_____

_____

_____

_____

_____

Teens' Stories

Gina, age 15, had always had a close relationship with her father. Her mother worked evenings, and Gina would often cook dinner for her father and younger sister, Anne. After she put Anne to bed, her father would sometimes come into her bedroom for intimate talks. Gina enjoyed this special time with him. When Gina was 10, her father began stroking and fondling her breasts. He assured her that this was normal for fathers to do with their daughters and that it was his role to teach her and make her feel good about her body.

At age 13, her father began having intercourse with her. At this point, Gina no longer believed her father's lies, but felt trapped. Her father became very possessive and controlling of her. He began to call her a "slut." He told her that her mother would never forgive her for seducing him and the family would be broken apart if she told. Gina was very confused, sad, and fearful. She didn't know what to do. One day, Gina came home and found her father wrestling with her little sister; his hands were sliding across Anne's buttocks. Gina became very angry and told her mother about the abuse that same day.

****

John, age 12, and Greg, age 13, were on a camping trip with their youth group and leader, Jerry, age 32. John and Greg had spent the day hiking and were assigned to the same tent together that night. Both boys were lying in their sleeping bags when Jerry entered their tent for a friendly chat. The boys had known Jerry for almost two years. Jerry sat next to John and began touching his hair and stroking his back. He told the boys that they were his two favorite group members and he wanted them to become his special assistants. Both boys were very excited. They felt very important. Both boys looked up to and trusted Jerry very much.

There were many more camping trips. Over time, Jerry began doing sexual things with them. He assured them that this was okay and that it was one of the membership requirements of being a "special assistant." John believed Jerry and thought this was okay. Greg was somewhat suspicious, but didn't feel he could say anything because people might think he was homosexual. John and Greg were too embarrassed to talk with each other about what had happened on these trips. Eventually, Greg did convince himself to tell his older brother who then helped him to tell their father.

****

Jean, age 14, often babysat for the Kingery kids. Mr. Kingery would drive her home after babysitting. He would tell Jean how pretty she was and how he imagined she must have lots of boyfriends. He would also tell her that his wife complained all the time about everything and that she didn't have time for him. He would say, " I sure wish I had a girlfriend like you. You really make me feel good when I'm with you." Jean would feel very flattered by Mr. Kingery's compliments. After a few months of this, Jean believed that he would like to be her boyfriend. He began kissing her good-night and then doing other sexual things with her. While Jean felt this was kind of strange, the compliments also made her feel very important and grown up. She was confused about what to do.

****

Remember the teen is never to blame for what the abuser does. Please talk to someone you trust if you believe that you are to blame for the abuse. These feelings can be hurtful and can get in the way of feeling better. It usually takes a while for these feelings to go away.

You deserve the time to heal!!!!!!!!

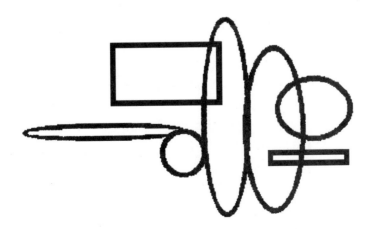

Can You Write Your Own Story?

_____

_____

_____

_____

_____

_____

_____

_____

_____

_____

_____

_____

_____

_____

What Other Teens Have Said

Elise, age 15

"I was only ten years old when it started. My uncle began living with me and my mom after my dad left. He used to come into my room at night while my mother was working. He started out just stroking my hair and face. It felt kind of comforting. I kind of thought it was funny, but I wasn't sure. It wasn't too long before he was climbing into bed with me and putting his fingers inside me; he also made me stroke him; I just didn't know what to do. I'd just lie there and pretend like I was sleeping. I'd sometimes find myself imagining I was somewhere else or not in my body...anywhere but there. I used to tell myself it didn't matter...that it was really no big deal. I mean, I knew kids who had it worse than me. I was tough and I thought I could handle it on my own. I kept myself very busy. I tried not to think about it and I was pretty good at it. The only thing was I had this great big knot in my stomach that felt like it was getting bigger and bigger. I remember feeling like I was soon going to disappear into it if it got any bigger. I finally asked for some help and talked to some people who really cared and helped me. It took a long time for that knot to go away. I guess...I think I finally dissolved that knot with my tears. It took me a long time, but I know now it was all worth it. I was worth it!"

John, age 16

"I never thought it could happen to me. I didn't even know it happened to guys. I didn't know any other guys who had been through the same thing or at least any guys who talked about it. I guess I thought it only happened to gays. And I always figured if anyone ever tried anything with me that I didn't like, I would beat them up or thrash them but he was bigger and stronger than me and...more importantly, he was a close friend of my dad. He was even married with kids. What a sick-o! While it was happening, I was 14 at the time. I couldn't even believe it was happening to me. Afterwards, I was afraid to tell anyone because I was afraid they might think I was weak or a homosexual. Worse than that...they might think that I wanted it to happen. That's what he told me. It was like a nightmare that only got worse when I closed my eyes. That was two years ago. I was in therapy for a year and group therapy with other guys. It took me a long time to realize that it wasn't my fault...that it wasn't something about me that caused it to happen. I'm still angry a lot...angry because of what I had to go through, but I know I'm going to be o.k. now. I've helped some other guys in the group. It helps a lot to know that someone else has been there and that you're not alone."

Maria, age 17

"My mother's boyfriend and I were always close. He referred to me as the daughter he'd always wanted; he never had any children of his own. I was 11 when he moved in with us. He began molesting me 8 days after he unpacked his stuff. My mother and him had been dating for 3 years, and he'd never ever laid a hand on me in any way that made me feel uncomfortable until he moved in. It all started one afternoon after I came home from school. My mother always ran her errands then and Jack wasn't working, so we'd usually talk or play a game together. He told me he had a new game for me. His game involved kissing me and rubbing up against me. I still can remember that sick feeling in the pit of my stomach when he forced my hand down his pants and started moaning. I was so scared. That night I locked my door. These episodes or "games" as he referred to them, continued. Each time he wanted me to do more and more until finally he began having intercourse with me. I didn't know what to do. My mother really loved him, and I knew she needed him to help pay the bills with his unemployment check. My mother wondered why I started crying when she told me they were planning on getting married. I hurt her when I absolutely refused to go shopping with her for her wedding dress.

I was devastated. I began staying in my room more and more. My grades dropped and I stopped taking care of myself. Looking back, I guess I was trying to tell my mother…or to tell anyone that something was really wrong. No one got the message. It went on for almost 2 years. I don't know…I kind of just stopped feeling anything…all my tears just sort of dried up and I didn't really feel alive or anything. I tried to go back to my normal life before the abuse, but I couldn't. I even began fantasizing about running away, killing him, or even killing myself. That's how bad I felt. At one point, I even remember thinking that it was my fault…if only I hadn't been born. One day I finally told my best friend and she talked me into telling our math teacher. I was so nervous…so afraid…afraid that maybe my mom wouldn't believe me when she found out. That's what he used to tell me, but she knew I had told my math teacher the truth. My mom was kind of upset at first because I hadn't told her sooner, but she really came through for me. At first, she felt like maybe it was her fault because she hadn't known or protected me. She hadn't had any idea what was going on. He had been so clever and tricky. I know that I'm o.k. now…that we're o.k. now. I'm a real survivor. That day my mom took me to the police station where we filed charges. Boy, was he surprised when the police came to question him and arrested him. He thought I'd never tell. Boy was he wrong."

A Test You Can't Fail

True or False?

1. *Teens are usually sexually abused by someone they know.*
   True_____   False_____

2. *Teens who sexually abuse may have been sexually abused themselves as children.*
   True_____   False_____

3. *Sexual abusers are always male.*
   True_____   False_____

4. *Only females are sexually abused.*
   True_____   False_____

5. *Teens who are sexually abused become homosexuals.*
   True_____   False_____

6. *Often, sexual abusers will stop abusing on their own.*
   True_____   False_____

7. *Usually, only one child within a family is sexually abused.*
   True_____   False_____

8. *Abusers will often blame their victim for the abuse.*
   True_____   False_____

9. *You can pick out sexual abusers by the way they look.*
   True_____   False_____

10. *Sexual abuse occurs exclusively in poor families.*
    True_____   False_____

Answers are on the following page.

Don't worry if you didn't answer them all correctly.
This exercise is intended to help you get some new information.

Answers

1. **True**. Kids and teens are almost always sexually abused by someone they know and trust.

2. **True**. People who sexually abuse kids were often sexually and/or physically abused themselves as kids. Sexual abusers often begin abusing children when they are teens. Some teens who have been hurt by sexual abuse choose to hurt others or get involved in abusive relationships. Remember teens can choose. They should not hurt others or become involved in abusive relationships. Therapy or getting help can make this choice easier.

3. **False**. Sexual abusers are not always males. Females also sexually abuse.

4. **False**. Not only females are sexually abused. Boys are also sexually abused. In fact, current research studies suggest that many more boys are being molested than had previously been thought.

5. **False**. Sexual abuse does not cause homosexuality. In other words, it does not follow that someone who is sexually abused will become homosexual. However, many teens who have been sexually abused experience some confusion and may worry about their sexual orientation.

6. **False**. Sexual abusers do not usually stop abusing on their own. Most abusers need help before they will stop abusing.

7. **False**. Many times, more than one child in the family is sexually abused. This is especially true when the abuser is a parent or relative.

8. **True**. Abusers use many tricks to get their victims to believe that they are responsible for the abuse or that they caused the abuse in some way.

9. **False**. Abusers can be male, female, attractive, sloppy, well-dressed, old, or young, etc.

10. **False**. Sexual abuse can occur in any family, regardless of level of income or education, and regardless of race, occupation, or religion. Sexual abusers are, in fact, often well respected and sometimes held up as leaders in their communities.

Factoids

* Both boys and girls are sexually abused.

* Sometimes boys have a harder time than girls telling anyone about the abuse.

* People who sexually abuse children can be either male or female.

* When teens are molested, it can be very confusing, especially if the sexual touching felt good.

* Kids often feel especially confused if the person abusing them is a parent, relative, close friend, or trusted person who does not threaten them but asks them to keep this their "special secret."

* Most kids are sexually abused by someone they know and trust.

Positive Messages

Here is a list of positive messages that might help you to feel better. It is important to challenge and replace any negative messages you may have about yourself as a result of the abuse. You may wish to say these messages out loud. It would be a good idea to say them daily.

1. I am absolutely not to blame.

2. What happened was not my fault.

3. Adults should never touch kids or teens in a sexual way.

4. I have a right to my own body and to decide who touches it.

5. There is nothing I did that caused the abuse.

6. I am not alone. Other kids and teens have had similar experiences.

7. People care about me.

8. I care about myself.

9. I can heal from the abuse.

10. The only person to blame for my being abused is the abuser.

**11. I have a right to all my feelings about the
abuse and the abuser.**

**12. I deserve to feel better, and I am going
to take good care of myself.**

Can you add some positive messages of your own?

_____

_____

_____

_____

_____

Write the message that you would most like to hear.

_____

_____

_____

_____

_____

Your Body

Often, teens who have been sexually abused feel ashamed of their bodies. They may be especially ashamed if the abuse felt pleasurable in any way. In addition, teens who have been abused often have special concerns and questions about their bodies. They may worry that their bodies have been hurt, or damaged, or are different because of the abuse. They sometimes worry that other people will be able to tell that they've been abused just by looking at them. This isn't true. Also, teens are often very concerned about contracting sexually transmitted diseases or becoming pregnant. It is very important to talk to a doctor or other adult about these concerns. It is essential that you have the appropriate medical information and care that you need.

The following books have very useful information about your body and sexuality:

Bell, R. (1981). *Changing bodies, changing lives.* New York, NY: Vintage Books.

Gordon, S. (1975). *The teenage survival book.* New York, NY: Random House Publishing.

Powell, E. (1991). *Talking back to sexual pressure: What to say.* Minneapolis, MN: CompCare Publishers.

****

Your body belongs to you. There are several exercises in this book that will help you to understand your body better. It is important to treat your body as you would a good friend and to take special care of it!

****

Feelings In Your Body

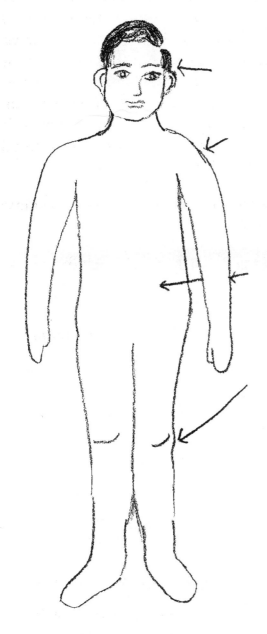

"My head is spinning."

"I've got a chip on my shoulder."

"I've got butterflies in my stomach."

"My knees are wobbly."

People often feel emotions in their bodies. Can you identify on the drawing where you have the following feelings in your body?

anger   embarrassment   sadness   fear   surprise

nervousness

Food for Thought

Many teens who have been sexually abused view their bodies in a distorted way. They sometimes imagine that they are fat, ugly, dirty, unattractive, etc. Teens who have been sexually abused often develop eating problems. They may find themselves preoccupied with food. They may attempt to numb their feelings or punish themselves by eating large quantities of food, or they may use food to soothe or reward themselves when they begin to feel emotional. Sometimes teens will eat large amounts of food in a compulsive way or binge and then force themselves to vomit. This eating disorder is called bulimia.

Other teens may find themselves preoccupied with a desire for thinness. They may become obsessed with calories and food intake. They may ignore hunger pangs, skip meals, and weigh themselves compulsively. They may view themselves as fat and flabby when in reality their bodies are normal or too thin. Often they experience guilt, anxiety, and self-hatred when they do eat. This eating disorder is called anorexia. Bulimia and anorexia are very unhealthy, dangerous, and can result in serious illness or even death.

****

List any changes in your eating habits since you were abused.

_____

_____

_____

_____

_____

_____

Answer the Following Questions:

Do you often find yourself intensely preoccupied with food?

Yes _____　　No_____

Do you find yourself eating to soothe or comfort yourself?

Yes_____　　No_____

Do you feel guilty when you eat?

Yes_____　　No_____

Do you find yourself obsessed with your body?

Yes_____　　No_____

Do you find yourself exercising compulsively?

Yes_____　　No_____

Do you ever make yourself throw up after you eat?

Yes_____　　No_____

Do you find yourself eating until you throw up?

Yes_____　　No_____

Do you find yourself thinking that you would be happy and have no problems if only you were thinner?

Yes_____　　No_____

Do you find yourself constantly on a diet, but no matter how much weight you lose…it is never enough?

Yes_____　　No_____

Do other people comment about how thin you are or comment that you never seem to eat?

Yes_____　　No_____

Do you think your body is ugly or dirty and deserves to be punished?

Yes_____　　No_____

Do you think if you gain weight, your body will no longer be attractive?

Yes_____　　No_____

Do you think that you will be protected from being abused again if you gain weight ?

Yes_____　　No_____

****

If you answered "yes" to any of these questions, please talk to your counselor. You may be developing an eating disorder, and you may need some help.

Relationships and Intimacy

During the teen years, relationships with others become increasingly important. Teens may be dating or may begin taking relationships with boyfriends or girlfriends more seriously. Dating can be fun and exciting, but it often has elements of confusion or insecurity. This is very normal.

Teens who have been sexually abused often encounter additional difficulties when dating. They may want to get close to another person, but may be afraid they will be hurt or betrayed. This may be especially true if the teen was abused by someone who they believed loved or cared about them. In this case, caring may now be equated with losing control and being hurt. Intimacy may be perceived as something very scary or threatening. They may allow themselves to get only so close, and then find themselves backing away. They may feel that not getting close to another person will protect or prevent them from getting hurt. Sometimes a teen who has been abused will go from relationship to relationship because it feels safer. Often, the teen will not be aware of these feelings, but may find himself or herself losing interest in a person when the involvement becomes at all serious.

Trusting others may be especially difficult for a while; this is a natural reaction to being abused. If someone likes or treats the teen as special, they may become afraid or panicky. It may remind them of their relationship with the abuser, especially if the abuser courted them and made them feel "special" before or during the abuse. It may also be hard for them to believe someone could genuinely think highly of or care about them because the abuse has left them feeling bad about themselves. Teens may also be afraid that if they become close, they will feel pressured to confide in their boyfriend or girlfriend about their abuse, and they may fear that the person will think badly of them or want to end the relationship. It is important for teens to know that they have a right to privacy and they have a choice about whom and when they tell about the abuse.

All of these feelings and reactions are normal responses to being sexually abused. It may take some time before you can feel safe and are able to trust or get close to someone. It is important to give yourself time to work through your feelings about the abuse. You may have many reactions, including a sense of loss, sadness, frustration, fear, and anger. Once again, it is important to remember that all of your feelings are okay and are there for a reason. It is also very helpful to get support and find someone you can talk with about these feelings. A group for teenage survivors can be important in this process. It can ease your isolation and remind you that you are not alone.

What kind of reactions have you experienced in dating or developing relationships?

S...e...x...u...a...l...i...t...y

We introduced the subject of your body and sexuality on page 22. As a teen, your body is going through many changes. Sexuality is a very complicated and individualized process. When a teen experiences puberty or a new awareness of his or her sexuality, many issues and feelings about abuse may be stirred up. Teens who have been sexually abused were often told by the abuser that they were seductive or that they wanted the abuse to happen. Sometimes teens have been rewarded or treated in a special way in exchange for the sexual abuse. This can be very confusing. They may then equate affection only with sexual touching or intercourse. They may have learned that they are valued as sex objects. They may believe the abuser and feel that others will care about them only if they go along with or invite sexual activity. This isn't true!

In many cases, the sexual touching may have seemed gentle or affectionate. Conversely, it may have been brutal or painful, and teens may feel that they had no control over their body and that they were simply used for another person's sexual gratification. Sexual abuse frequently leaves a person feeling degraded and humiliated. It is an act of violence and an abuse of power by the abuser. As a result of this trauma, teens may feel they no longer have any control over their bodies and may have difficulty knowing how to respond to sexual overtures. There may be much confusion about when or how to be sexually active.

In addition to concerns about sexual activity, teens often feel sad, cheated, and angry because they didn't choose with whom their first sexual experience took place. They were forced to have a sexual experience at an early age without any regard for their feelings. Teens are entitled to their feelings. It is true that abused teens were cheated. They were exposed to sexuality before they were ready or able to make that decision. However, you still have the right and opportunity to choose future sexual relationships that are caring and mutual.

You may want to do some further reading on this topic. These books have useful information.

Your Body and Sexuality

Bell, R. (1981). *Changing bodies, changing lives.* New York, NY: Vintage Books.

Gordon, S. (1975). *The teenage survival book.* New York, NY: Random House Publishing.

Powell, E. (1991). *Talking back to sexual pressure: What to say.* Minneapolis, MN: CompCare Publishers.

What kinds of questions or concerns do you have about being sexually active?

_____

_____

_____

_____

_____

_____

_____

_____

_____

_____

_____

_____

_____

_____

Body Talk

Ways to feel good about your body:

1. Do some stretching exercises.

2. Lie down and breathe deeply. Feel your breath and imagine it calming your entire body.

3. Put on some music. Move to the music.

4. Get some exercise: swim, run, go for a nature walk.

5. Join a movement class: dance, martial arts, gymnastics, etc.

6. Get involved in a sport.

Add some others if you want.

1. _____

2. _____

3. _____

4. _____

5. _____

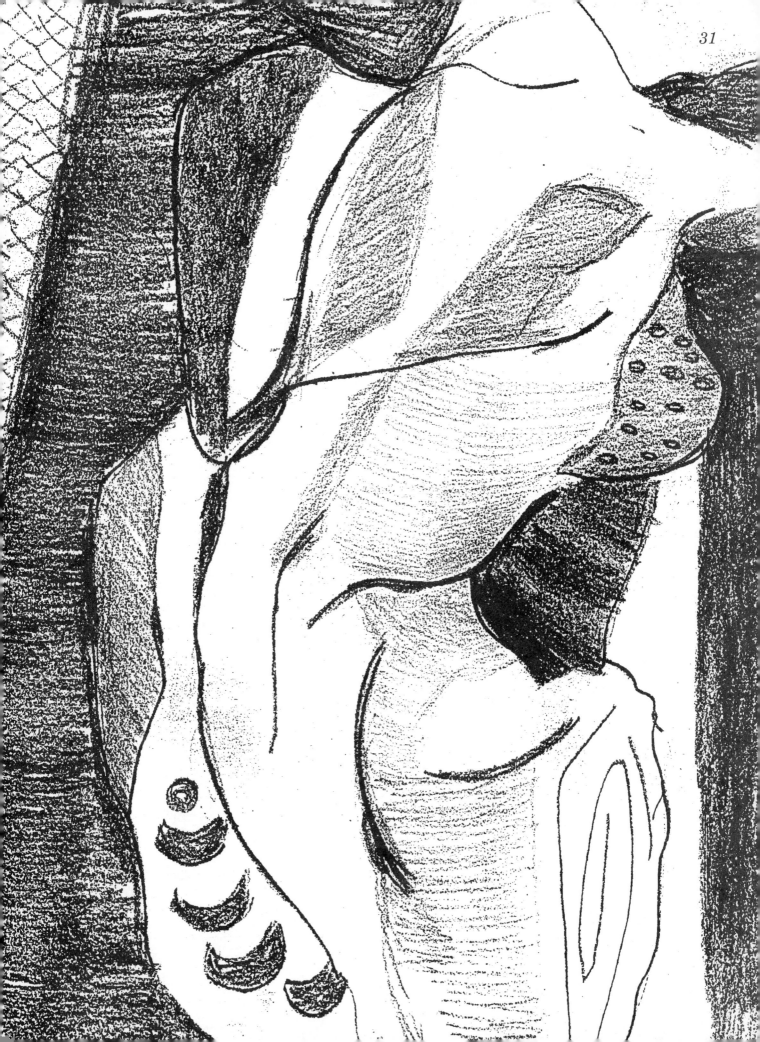

I Heard It...

We all receive messages about ourselves from our families, peers, religious groups, ethnic groups, and society. Sometimes these messages are positive and can help us to feel good about ourselves. However, if these messages are negative and we accept them as true, we may feel bad about ourselves. Negative messages should be challenged. This exercise is designed to help you identify and be aware of these messages and where they come from.

Messages I Have Heard

(About being me)

The message	Who said it?	+ or -	How I feel
1.			
2.			
3			
4.			
5.			

(About my body)

The message	Who said it?	+ or -	How I feel
1.			
2.			
3			
4.			
5.			

(About being a male or female in this society)

The message	Who said it?	+ or -	How I feel
1.			
2.			
3			
4.			
5.			

(About other people)

The message	Who said it?	+ or -	How I feel
1.			
2.			
3			
4.			
5.			

Messages I Would Like To Hear

What are the messages you would like to hear? You may think about replacing some of the messages on the previous pages if they are negative. You may also want to add some of your own. What messages would enhance your self-esteem or help you to feel better about yourself?

Messages I Want To Hear

(About being me)

1. _____

2. _____

3. _____

4. _____

5. _____

(About my body)

1. _____

2. _____

3. _____

4. _____

5. _____

Messages I Want To Hear

(About being a male or female in this society)

1. _____

2. _____

3. _____

4. _____

5. _____

(About other people)

1. _____

2. _____

3. _____

4. _____

5. _____

Creative Visualization:
Tripping Without Alcohol or Drugs

You might wish to do this with someone else or by yourself.

To begin: get in a very comfortable position, take some deep breaths, close your eyes, and relax. You could also put on some of your favorite music.

Imagine yourself somewhere very beautiful and peaceful. It may be somewhere you've really been, or it may be a place in your imagination. Is it a lush green park, forest, or a mountain top with a gushing stream or waterfall? It might be near the ocean or a desert with cactus flowers. Maybe it's in the woods somewhere with the smell of pine trees. Maybe it's a special place in your home. You pick the place.

Are you alone or is there a close friend or family member there with you? Continue taking deep breaths and relax your entire body. This is a place where you feel relaxed, calm, safe, and nurtured. It is your place...a place where tensions are soothed away. What are you doing in this place? Are you resting, sitting, strolling, or briskly walking? What are the sights, the smells, the sounds? It is your place...your refuge. Take your time and allow yourself to rest here for awhile.

***Now that you've found and experienced this place,
remember you carry it with you.***

You can go to your special place whenever you want.

It is a place for you to heal!

Anger

Survivors often react to being sexually abused by becoming angry. Anger is a normal response to being abused. It can be very healing if it is not used to mask other feelings such as grief, loss, powerlessness, and isolation. You have a right to be angry about what happened to you. While it is okay to be angry, it is not okay to express your anger by hurting yourself or someone else. It is very important to find safe ways to express your anger.

Ways to safely express your anger:

1. Write a poem or song expressing your anger.

2. Write a letter expressing your anger. After you've written the letter, you may or may not decide to mail it.

3. Get some exercise: go for a run or hit a ball against a wall.

4. Do a silent scream.

5. Talk with someone you trust about your anger.

6. Plan out in your imagination or tape record what you would want to say to the person who abused you.

7. Punch pillows.

8. Hit a punching bag.

9. Make a drawing or sculpture about your anger.

10. Write in a journal.

What else would you add?

_____

_____

_____

_____

Anger Turned Inward

When anger is not expressed or acknowledged, it is stuffed down and treated as if it doesn't exist. This stuffing down of anger often leads to depression. People who don't let themselves have angry feelings often turn these feelings against themselves. Eventually, feelings that have been stuffed down do come out. Many times they can come out in ways that are not helpful. For example, some teens who tell themselves they are not angry about the abuse find themselves:

-crying for no apparent reason.
-wanting or trying to hurt themselves.
- being in a relationship with someone who treats them poorly.
-feeling bad about themselves.
-crawling into a shell and withdrawing from people.
-drinking or using drugs to numb their feelings.
-overeating or depriving themselves of food.

*Can you think of some other things teens might experience
from stuffing their feelings and pretending that they don't exist?*

_____

_____

_____

_____

_____

_____

_____

*Pay attention to all of your feelings;
they are important.*

Teens' Letters

Dear Mike,

I hate you for what you did to the other guys and me. I know you did it to them, too, because we finally got up the nerve to ask each other and to talk about it. You tricked each of us into believing that we were special to you. We've all decided that you're scum and we hope you get yours, too.

John

Dear Bill,

I despise you for what you did to me. Sometimes I wish you'd get caught and go to jail for it. But it's strange. I miss you too sometimes. I felt like that after getting that letter from you last week saying all those good things about me. It's really confusing. I don't know what to think. I know I should hate you. I hope you'll answer this letter.

Buddy

(Sometimes teens have both good and bad feelings about the person who abused them. Buddy thought that Bill was a good friend because he took him places, treated him well, and made him feel special. Buddy was hurt and angry about the abuse, but still missed Bill. It's normal and okay to have different feelings at the same time.)

Maria,

I'm writing to let you know that I remember that sexual stuff you used to do with Marty and me when you babysat us. We were too little then to know it was wrong. We're planning to go to the police and have you investigated because we figure you're probably doing the same stuff with your kids. What you did was abuse and we plan to put a stop to it!

Natalie

Dear Mom,

I'll get right to the point. I'm furious that you let dad molest me and you never did anything to stop it. You even walked into the bedroom one time when he was on top of me. So don't try to say you don't remember. It's all your fault I feel the way I do. I can't get a boyfriend. I'm flunking out in school and sometimes I feel like I want to kill myself. I don't understand why you didn't stop him. I know you could have. I don't think I'll ever be able to come back home and face you again.

Your ex-daughter,

Maria

Letter to the Abuser

To: _____   Date: _____

From: _____

    There are a lot of things I want to say to you! I used to feel _____

_____

_____

_____

_____. After you began to abuse me, I felt

_____

_____

_____

I thought _____

_____

_____

_____

When I think of what you did to me, I feel _____

_____

_____

_____

If you ever try to molest me again, I will _____

_____

_____

_____

I am safe now because _____

_____

_____

_____

Signed: _____

Write your own letter to the person who abused you. Say whatever you feel like saying:

Date: _____

_____

_____

_____

_____

_____

_____

_____

_____

_____

_____

_____

_____

_____

_____

_____

_____

More Letters

Write a letter to someone you've told about the abuse.

Date: _____

Dear _____,

When I told you about the abuse, _____
_____
_____
_____

I want to let you know that _____
_____
_____
_____

I know that you feel _____
_____
_____
_____

I wish _____
_____
_____
_____

I hope that you and I _____
_____
_____
_____

Sincerely,

_____

P.S.

_____
_____

Write a letter to another teen who has been sexually abused. Give the teen advice.

Date: _____

Dear _____,

    I am so sorry to hear about what happened to you. I understand because _____

_____

_____

When it happened to me, I felt _____

_____

_____

I felt better when _____

_____

_____

My advice is _____

_____

_____

_____

I understand what you're going through is really hard because _____

_____

_____

_____

I wanted to write this letter to let you know that you are not alone. I hope my advice will help you.

Sincerely,

_____

P.S.

_____

_____

Letter From the Abuser

In order to write this letter, pretend you are the person who abused you.
What would you like the abuser to say to you?

Date: _____

Dear _____,

    I have so many things I need to say to you. For example, _____

_____

_____

_____

_____

I have hurt you so much. It was entirely my fault. In order to say I'm sorry_____

_____

_____

_____

_____

I know that I _____

_____

_____

_____

_____

I know that you may never be able to forgive me.

Sincerely,

_____

P.S.

_____

_____

Your Day in Court

What sentence would you like your abuser to have?

Date: _____

Judge's Name: _____

Defendant: (the person who sexually abused you)

_____

For the crime of: _____

The defendant is sentenced to:

_____

_____

and must _____

_____

_____to make restitution for this crime.

Being Hurt and Hurting Yourself

Sometimes teens who are sexually abused are hurt, confused, and angry. They may try to express these feelings by hurting themselves. The confused feelings may come out in a number of ways. For example teens may become sexually active before they are ready, run away from home, get into gangs, put themselves into dangerous situations, use drugs or alcohol, cut themselves, or make suicide attempts.

Bob, age 14, had been molested by his father's close friend since he was 7 years old. He never told anyone because he was afraid people might think he was strange or that there was something wrong with him. Over time, he became more and more isolated and would spend a lot of time in his room alone. As a teen he began drinking with his friends every time they were together. After awhile he found that he wanted to drink every day. He began to do poorly in school and constantly thought about running away from home. A couple of times he felt so down that he thought about ending his life.

Bob began attending a group for teens at his school. Much to his surprise, he discovered that two other boys in the group had also been molested. He began to understand that his self-destructive behavior was a reaction to his feelings about being abused. His group counselor helped him to tell his parents about the abuse. As he was working out these feelings, he noticed that he no longer needed or wanted to drink. He also found it easier to make new friends again, and his school work improved significantly.

* *

Vivian was molested between the ages of 6 and 9 by her female babysitter. The babysitter told Vivian that her mother wouldn't be able to go to work and would lose her job if she told anyone about the abuse. At age 15, Vivian found herself angry much of the time. She picked fights almost every day and would be sent to the office at least once a week. At home, Vivian often found herself bursting into tears for no apparent reason. She was upset and confused most of the time. On several occasions, she was very preoccupied with negative thoughts about herself. Once she got hit by a car while riding her bicycle, and another time she seriously cut her finger while preparing dinner.

Vivian was alarmed by these incidents and decided she must tell someone about the abuse. She forced herself to confide in the school principal, who was about to suspend her. The principal helped her to talk to her mother about the abuse. He also referred her to the school social worker, who helped her to understand the connection between her feelings about the abuse and her self- destructive behavior. After a couple of months of working with the school social worker, Vivian began to feel better about herself.

Often, teens who don't feel good about themselves find ways of hurting or punishing themselves. It is very important to pay close attention to ways you may be putting yourself in risky or dangerous situations.

Are there times...

You wanted to or did hurt yourself? (Running away, getting into unhealthy or abusive relationships/friendships, putting yourself in dangerous situations.) Tell how:

_____

_____

_____

You found yourself involved in sexual relationships that were not meaningful? Comment if you'd like:

_____

_____

_____

You found yourself having lots of accidents? Tell what kind and how serious they were:

_____

_____

_____

You found yourself using drugs or alcohol? Tell about your use:

_____

_____

_____

You wanted to stop living or tried to kill yourself? Tell how:

_____

_____

_____

It is very important to talk about these feelings and behaviors with a therapist or trusted adult, especially if you have the urge to hurt yourself.

50

Being Hurt and Hurting Others

Most teens who were sexually abused experience themselves as powerless. The abuse may have left them feeling hurt, angry, damaged, and confused. As a result, they may have the urge to or may put themselves in the position to do to others what was done to them. Many of these feelings come out in ways that are harmful to others, such as manipulating or exploiting others, being mean, cruel, or verbally abusive, being physically aggressive, or sexually approaching younger kids.

Jose and Lydia, age 16, had both been sexually abused as children. They frequently babysat for a neighborhood family. Jose would find himself becoming sexually aroused each time he gave the 2 year old her bath. He began suggesting to Lydia that they fondle the child while drying her off. Lydia agreed, but the more they talked about it, the more they realized that they were having some reactions to their own sexual abuse. Jose and Lydia realized that touching the child would be inappropriate. Fortunately, they were able to help each other not to act on their urges.

Are there times...

You found yourself being manipulative with others? Tell how:

_____

_____

_____

You found yourself being mean, cruel, or verbally abusive? Tell about those times:

_____

_____

_____

You found yourself being physically aggressive with others? Tell how:

_____

_____

_____

You had the urge to approach a younger kid in a sexual way? Tell about that:

_____

_____

_____

S.O.S...Be on the Lookout

Many teens who were molested as children often find themselves being re-victimized or taken advantage of. For example,

Seventeen year old Anna, who had been abused by her uncle, met Tom, who flattered and charmed her. After their third date, he took her to his apartment and pressured her to have sex. When she told him that she didn't feel ready, he held her down and raped her. Anna was wise enough to know that this shouldn't have happened, and she reported him to the police.

What do you think Anna was thinking that helped her to be assertive and take appropriate action?

_____

_____

_____

Greg, age sixteen, who had been molested by his mother, was dating Tina and liked her a lot. Tina did nothing but put him down, order him around, and constantly tell him he was stupid. While Greg didn't like her behavior, he was afraid that no other girl would be attracted to him; he stayed in the relationship, and she became more abusive over time.

What do you think Greg needs to do in order to be assertive in this relationship?

_____

_____

_____

Thirteen year old Maria, who had been sexually abused by a male teacher, often found herself sexually involved with older men. While she was looking for affection and caring, she usually ended up feeling used and exploited. Eventually, Maria met Jim, who was her own age. They became very good friends and cared about one another. She learned from this relationship that sex and affection were not one and the same thing.

What do you think Maria learned about the difference between sex, affection, and caring?

_____

_____

_____

It would be good to think about how you would like to be treated so that your privacy and boundaries are respected and so that you get the love and affection you deserve. You may want to develop a list of questions to ask yourself. That will help you pay close attention to the way others talk to you and treat you.

In relationships...

1. Do you feel respected and cared about?

   Does the other person listen to you or only talk about themselves?

   Does the other person genuinely want to know who you are?

2. Do you find yourself feeling pressured sexually against your wishes?

   Do you worry that you won't be liked if you don't give in?

3. Do you find yourself looking for affection through sexual behavior?

4. Do you find yourself in situations where you end up feeling used and exploited or feeling valued and appreciated?

What questions would you add?

_____

_____

_____

_____

_____

_____

Teens' Poems

You crept into my room at night
I felt my body tense up tight.
I pretended to be asleep
And now I pray my soul to keep.
I dared not cry
You would tell mom it was a lie.
No one knows the pain I feel
I'm not sure I'll ever heal.

The Dark Night

Rage and fury
Pain to bury
Lustful sinner that you are
Insides filled with tar
Rage and fury
Pain to bury
I can't forgive you
I won't forgive you
sinner that you are.

The Secret

The secret is out
I want to shout
It's not okay what you did to me
But I am free
The secret is out at last
The abuse is in the past
My scars will heal
and I can start to feel
The secret is out
Glory, glory hallelujah

Thief of Childhood

My dreams were fractured
Eyes of ice, you pierced my soul
With each grasp of your hand
i felt my youth crumble away
i was an instrument of your fancy
Affection had nothing to do with it
now liars get their just desserts...I know!

Write a poem of your own

Daily News

Advice Column

You are the editor for the paper. Teens write to you for advice. What would you tell these teens to do?

My baseball coach has been doing sexual things with me. I'm very confused and don't know what I should do. He has been a really good coach and helped me to win the "Best Player of the Year" award at school. Please help me to decide what I need to do.

Embarrassed and confused in Colorado,

John

_____

_____

_____

My friend Mary is a fellow member of the cheerleading squad. Last week she asked me if my dad ever does sexual things with me. I told her no. I'm not sure what to think about Mary's question. I'm afraid something is wrong. What should I say or ask Mary? I think she needs my help.

A concerned friend,

Natasha

_____

_____

_____

My boyfriend, Frank, gave me his ring to wear on Friday. On Saturday he cancelled our date because he said he had to work. I found out a few days later that a friend of mine saw him out with another girl on Saturday. I don't think he saw my friend. Can you give me some ideas about what to do?

Upset and distrustful,

Tina

_____

_____

_____

How would you describe yourself:

after the abuse ended

_____

_____

_____

_____

_____

_____

_____

now

_____

_____

_____

_____

_____

_____

_____

Ways To Get a Grip:

Things to do when feeling afraid or overwhelmed:

1. Take several deep breaths.

2. Seek out a family member or a special friend to talk to.

3. Say a prayer.

4. Use your visualization exercise.

5. Remember your positive messages.

6. Listen to some music that you like.

7. Take a walk, play a game, or do some exercise that will help your body to relieve tension.

8. Write in your journal.

9. Talk with your therapist.

What else works for you?

_____

_____

_____

_____

_____

_____

Rap or Write

Write a rap song or a story about how you are healing from your abuse.

The Me I May or May Not Know

Getting to know yourself can be a lot of fun. It can help you to find things that you really enjoy and like to do. It can help you to gain an understanding and appreciation of yourself.

1. What are some things that you like to do for fun?

_____

_____

_____

2. What are some things that you don't like to do?

_____

_____

_____

3. What are some things that you like about yourself?

_____

_____

_____

4. Who is someone you really admire and why?

_____

_____

_____

5. What is your favorite sport? Why?

_____

_____

_____

6. What is your favorite thing to do in your spare time?

_____

_____

_____

7. Who is your best friend? Why?

_____

_____

_____

8. Who are some other friends? Tell why:

_____

_____

_____

9. What kinds of things upset you?

_____

_____

_____

10. What kinds of things do you get enthusiastic about?

_____

_____

_____

11. What do you worry about most?

_____

_____

_____

12. When and where do you feel the safest? What helps to make it feel safe?

_____

_____

_____

13. What do you like to daydream about?

_____

_____

_____

14. If you had an unexpected day off from school, how would you spend it?

_____

_____

_____

15. List three hobbies or interests.

_____

_____

_____

Measuring Scale:

This measuring scale is being repeated here so that you can be aware of any changes in your thinking, feeling, or behavior. It will help you to understand more about yourself. You might wish to discuss some of these with your therapist.

Circle one:

I feel scared.	Always	Most of the time	Sometimes	Never
I like myself.	Always	Most of the time	Sometimes	Never
I feel sad.	Always	Most of the time	Sometimes	Never
I'm afraid.	Always	Most of the time	Sometimes	Never
I'm embarrassed.	Always	Most of the time	Sometimes	Never
I feel angry.	Always	Most of the time	Sometimes	Never
I'm happy.	Always	Most of the time	Sometimes	Never
I get upset.	Always	Most of the time	Sometimes	Never
I have nightmares.	Always	Most of the time	Sometimes	Never
I am a good person.	Always	Most of the time	Sometimes	Never
I'm shy.	Always	Most of the time	Sometimes	Never
I have friends.	Always	Most of the time	Sometimes	Never
I like other teens.	Always	Most of the time	Sometimes	Never
My family likes me.	Always	Most of the time	Sometimes	Never
I would be a good friend to have.	Always	Most of the time	Sometimes	Never
I'm excited about growing up.	Always	Most of the time	Sometimes	Never
I like my body.	Always	Most of the time	Sometimes	Never

I worry about how well other teens like me.	Always	Most of the time	Sometimes	Never
I feel attractive.	Always	Most of the time	Sometimes	Never
I feel fat.	Always	Most of the time	Sometimes	Never
I worry about having a boyfriend/girlfriend.	Always	Most of the time	Sometimes	Never
My friends like me.	Always	Most of the time	Sometimes	Never
I feel guilty when I eat.	Always	Most of the time	Sometimes	Never
I'm intelligent.	Always	Most of the time	Sometimes	Never
I'm creative.	Always	Most of the time	Sometimes	Never
I have a good sense of humor.	Always	Most of the time	Sometimes	Never
I am overly sensitive.	Always	Most of the time	Sometimes	Never
I cry.	Always	Most of the time	Sometimes	Never
I am self-conscious.	Always	Most of the time	Sometimes	Never
Other people think highly of me.	Always	Most of the time	Sometimes	Never
I get bored.	Always	Most of the time	Sometimes	Never
I prefer being alone to being with others.	Always	Most of the time	Sometimes	Never
I'm preoccupied with negative thoughts about myself.	Always	Most of the time	Sometimes	Never
I think about hurting myself.	Always	Most of the time	Sometimes	Never
I'd like to have more friends.	Always	Most of the time	Sometimes	Never
Adults care about me.	Always	Most of the time	Sometimes	Never

A Journal

A journal is like a diary. It is a creative way to express your thoughts and feelings. It provides a special and private place for you to keep track of where you've been and where you're going. You may feel a little awkward at first writing in your journal, but the more you write, the easier it will become. Remember, there is no one else just like you. Writing in a journal will show your unique and special way of looking at yourself and your life.

You may wish to decorate a cover for your journal.

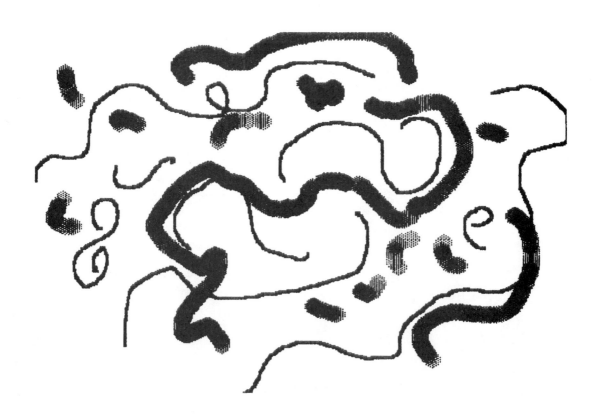

My

Journal

Name: _____

My Journal

Record the date each time you write in your journal.

_____

_____

_____

_____

_____

_____

_____

_____

_____

_____

_____

_____

_____

_____

_____

_____

_____

(It would be helpful if you could get a special notebook to use for your journal.
You can also put pictures in your journal.)

Imagine

Imagine you are looking into your future.
What do you see for yourself?

What Do You See in This Picture?

Knowing What You Feel

All feelings are natural and normal. Feelings are not good or bad; they are not right or wrong. Feelings help you to learn about yourself. If you pay attention to your feelings, you will know who you are...what you like...what you don't like...what kind of people and situations make you feel sad, scared, happy, angry, lonely, or joyful.

Many times teens who have been abused numb themselves to their feelings as a way of coping. Sometimes they develop a very narrow range of emotions. A healing journey is a chance to discover many of the feelings that you have not previously recognized.

Feeling Associations

What's the first thing that comes to your mind for each of these feelings? Your response can be one word, a few words, or a sentence.

Don't censor yourself!

Content _____

Powerless _____

Angry _____

Amazed _____

Fearful_____

Hurried _____

Powerful _____

Frustrated _____

Afraid_____

Excited_____

Discouraged _____

Happy _____

Nervous _____

Jealous _____

Goofy _____

Ashamed _____

Proud _____

Worried _____

Puzzled _____

Thrilled _____

Sad _____

Love _____

Hate _____

Generous _____

Disappointed _____

Spellbound _____

Fulfilled _____

Sticky Situations

The situations on the next page can be difficult, and there are no right or wrong answers. You might find yourself having many different feelings if you were in any of these situations. Remember…feelings are not right or wrong, and you are entitled to all of your feelings. Making decisions about situations can often be difficult. It is important to be true to yourself and do what you feel and think is right. Many times it can be helpful to talk with someone about your feelings.

How would you feel and what would you do if...

1. You saw your best friend out with your boyfriend/girlfriend? _____

_____

_____

_____

2. You saw someone stealing your bike from in front of the grocery store?

_____

_____

_____

_____

3. You and your best friend auditioned for a part in a play and your best friend got the part? _____

_____

_____

_____

You got the part? _____

_____

_____

_____

4. You had a date scheduled and another friend invited you to a concert that you wanted to attend that same night? _____

_____

_____

_____

5. You overheard your parents having a fight? _____

_____

_____

_____

Feeling Completion

If you aren't "burned out" on feelings, try these.

I like it when _____

I get upset when _____

I feel the best when _____

I am _____

I get angry when _____

My dad is _____

My mom is _____

I don't want to _____

I like myself when _____

I cry when _____

The thing I like most about myself is _____

I get sad when _____

I feel ready to _____

I think I can _____

I know I can _____

My feelings get hurt when _____

Nobody understands that _____

I feel confused when _____

I feel safe when _____

I don't like _____

My family is _____

I have fun when _____

My biggest fear is _____

I don't talk about_____

I feel ashamed when _____

When I grow up _____

I'm glad to be me because _____

I am great because _____

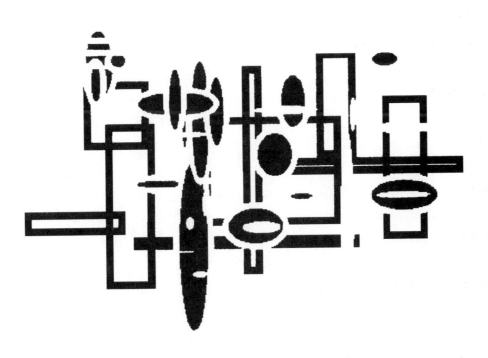

Take a Break

It's important to take time to relax and to give yourself a break.
Can you unscramble these feeling words?

VETSISNIE   _____

VENSOUR   _____

LYNOEL   _____

FONCESUD   _____

TIXEDCE   _____

NYGRA   _____

FUN QUIZ

1. Name three rock groups you wish you had never heard.

_____

_____

2. What is your favorite t.v. show?

_____

_____

3. What is your favorite movie?

_____

_____

4. What is your favorite song?

_____

_____

6. Who is your favorite character from a book?

_____

_____

7. What is the best book you have ever read?

_____

_____

ANSWERS: sensitive, nervous, lonely, confused, excited, angry

Crossword Puzzle

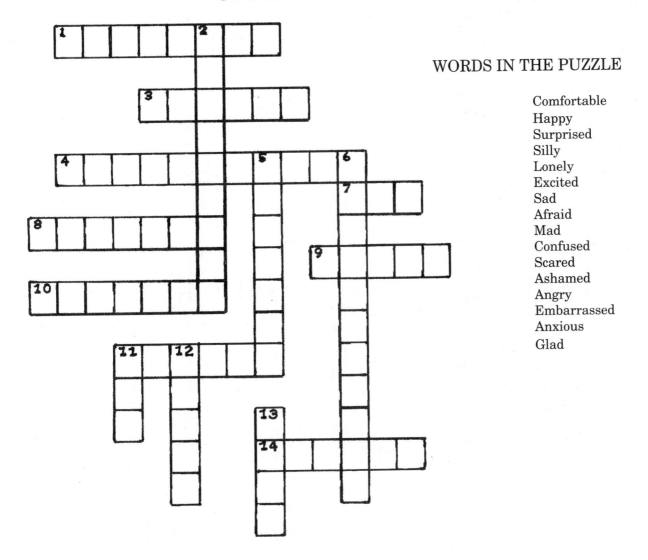

WORDS IN THE PUZZLE

Comfortable
Happy
Surprised
Silly
Lonely
Excited
Sad
Afraid
Mad
Confused
Scared
Ashamed
Angry
Embarrassed
Anxious
Glad

Across

1. Feeling lost or as if you don't know what direction to take.
3. Feeling scared or frightened.
4. Feeling at ease and like you fit in.
7. Angry.
8. Nervous or tense. Sometimes it means excited.
9. Glad or pleased.
10. Feeling like you can't wait for a surprise.
11. Frightened.
14. Feeling alone and sad.

Down

2. Excited by something you didn't expect.
5. Feeling embarrassed, guilty, or like you've done something wrong.
6. Feeling self-conscious or like you've done something silly.
11. Feeling depressed or down in the dumps.
12. Feeling upset and mad.
13. Happy.

Crossword Puzzle Key

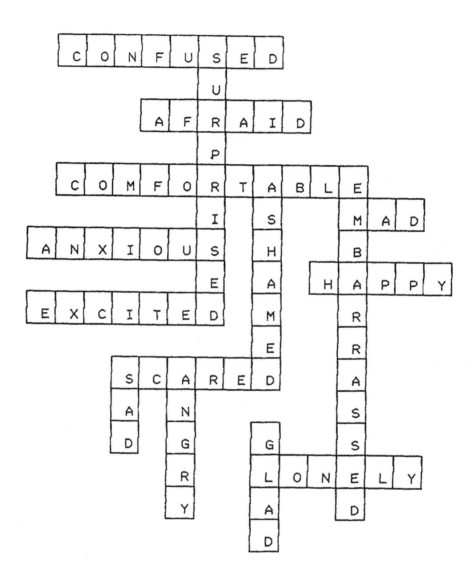

Word Search

Find and circle the words below in this feeling puzzle. (Words can be found backwards, forwards, horizontally, vertically, and diagonally.)

The key to the puzzle is on the next page.

HAPPY SHY ANXIOUS SAD SILLY ANGRY CONFUSED UPSET

AFRAID LONELY SMART SURPRISED SPECIAL GLAD

```
G  L  A  D  O  S  U  R  P  R  I  S  E  D
X  O  N  I  K  M  P  O  I  L  U  D  N  W
D  N  G  A  L  A  H  Z  V  Z  Z  P  A  A
F  E  R  R  P  R  O  H  P  O  M  L  O  I
P  L  Y  F  P  T  Z  C  I  O  N  T  O  I
O  Y  I  A  N  X  I  O  U  S  K  Y  E  S
U  I  K  T  N  R  M  V  S  U  J  K  O  A
P  E  X  O  C  G  O  M  O  V  L  G  P  D
S  H  Y  A  O  O  R  P  U  H  A  P  P  Y
E  C  K  I  P  Q  N  Y  O  Z  P  M  T  I
T  O  U  J  S  M  T  F  S  I  O  Z  O  P
Y  L  L  I  S  O  V  A  U  F  L  O  D  K
I  E  O  P  U  H  W  L  Y  S  T  L  G  L
A  K  M  L  K  L  Z  H  D  E  E  D  K  L
O  S  L  A  I  C  E  P  S  F  R  D  E  N
P  Z  V  E  O  M  M  O  A  L  Z  X  O  P
```

Key to Word Search

```
G  (L  A  D)  O  (S  U  R  P  R  I  S  E  D)  D
X   O  N   I  K   M  P  O  I  L  U  D  N     W
D   N  G   A  L   A  H  Z  V  Z  Z  P  A     A
F   E  R   R  P   R  O  H  P  O  M  L  O     I
P   L  Y   F  P   T  Z  C  I  O  N  T  O     I
O   Y  I   A  N  X  I  O  U  S)  K  Y  E    (S
U   I  K   T  N  R  M  V  S  U  J  K  O      A
P   E  X   O  C  G  O  M  O  V  L  G  P      D)
S  (H  Y)  A  O  R  P  U (H  A  P  P  Y)
E   C  K   I  P  Q  N  Y  O  Z  P  M  T      I
T   O  U   J  S  M  T  F  S  I  O  Z  O      P
Y)  L  L   I  S) O  V  A  U  F  L  O  D  K   L
I   E  O   P  U  H  W  L  Y  S  T  L  G      L
A   K  M   L  K  L  Z  H  D  E  E  D  K      L
O   S (L   A  I  C  E  P  S) F  R  D  E   N
P   Z  V   E  O  M  M  O  A  L  Z  X  O      P
```

Self-Development: Don't Put Me Down!

Self-esteem refers to how people feel about themselves. Some people accept themselves and are comfortable being who they are, whereas others are very critical of themselves. Self-esteem refers to how much a person feels valued and important.

Much of people's sense of self-esteem depends on the type of messages they were given while growing up. Children who are given the message that they are worthwhile, smart, and creative usually grow up feeling confident. On the other hand, children who are given negative messages about themselves often grow up feeling insecure and doubting themselves. Many people store these messages in their memories and believe them to be true. It is often very difficult to undo negative messages, but it can be done. It takes time.

Teens who have been sexually abused often become preoccupied with negative messages about themselves. None of these negative messages is true, and they should be challenged.

Remember: Being abused does not define who you are,
but rather something that has happened to you.

You can choose to replace negative messages with messages that reflect who you are now and help you to appreciate your strengths. One other thing to remember is that how you feel about yourself will change over time as you grow and develop. It will be like a journey with many exciting paths of discovery. On your journey, you will learn much about yourself, about others, and about the world you live in.

The exercise on the next page will help you on your journey

to learning about yourself.

How I See Myself

Put a check next to the words that best describe you.

___Sincere   ___Angry   ___Envious

___Friendly   ___Dishonest   ___Humorous

___Shy   ___Honest   ___Compassionate

___Courageous   ___Ambitious   ___Caring

___Smart   ___Funny   ___Intelligent

___Mean   ___Mopey   ___Hard working

___Kind   ___Sensitive   ___Sloppy

___Rude   ___Fearful   ___Strong

___Helpful   ___Bold   ___Energetic

___Successful   ___Introverted ___Extroverted

Most people see both negative and positive qualities in themselves. Sometimes you will find yourself behaving, feeling, or thinking differently depending on the situation you are in or the people you are with. Remember you can always change any attitude or behavior about yourself that you would like to be different.

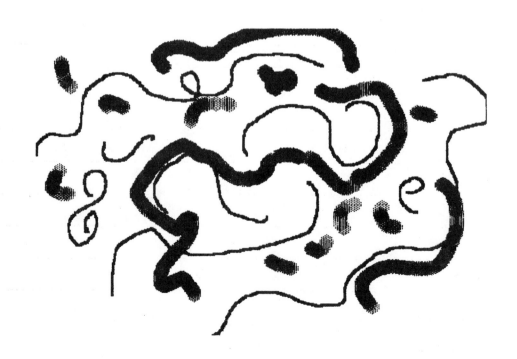

Give Yourself Credit

Sometimes people aren't used to giving themselves positive messages or credit for the things they can do well. This exercise might be difficult or may make you feel a little uncomfortable. Do the best you can and remember that you are a good, worthwhile person and that you deserve to feel good about yourself!

Make a list of all the things you like about yourself:

_____

_____

_____

_____

_____

Make a list of all the things you can do well:

_____

_____

_____

_____

_____

Make a list of skills you would like to develop:

_____

_____

_____

_____

_____

Promoting Yourself

Some of the questions frequently asked of people applying for a job are:

Name _____

Date _____

What special skills and experiences do you have?

_____

_____

_____

_____

What are your hobbies and interests?

_____

_____

_____

_____

_____

What have you accomplished that you are proud of?

_____

_____

_____

_____

_____

_____

_____

What are your career interests or plans?

_____

_____

_____

_____

_____

_____

_____

How do you learn best? What helps you to learn?

_____

_____

_____

_____

What kinds of questions do you have for the employer?

_____

_____

_____

_____

_____

_____

(You might wish to role play or write your answers.)

Getting There

Goals and Objectives

Setting goals is an aid to accomplishing your future plans. Goals are like targets or end zones. Objectives are the specific steps which you need to take in order to reach the end point or accomplish the goal. Here are some examples:

Goal: **To become a long-distance runner and eventually compete in the Olympics.**

Objective: Begin running 1 mile each day and gradually increase mileage and stamina.

Objective: Engage in weight lifting for 30 minutes 3 to 5 times per week.

Objective: Swim 30 laps 3 to 4 times per week.

Goal: **To get a part in the annual school play.**

Objective: Sign up for a class in acting at school.

Objective: Get together with friends and practice reading and memorizing parts.

Objective: Attend some theater productions.

Objective: Read a book on acting.

Goal: **To learn how to cook.**

Objective: Watch someone cook.

Objective: Make a list of things I'd like to learn to cook.

Objective: Get a book with recipes. Pick a recipe that is fairly simple to start with.

Objective: Purchase ingredients.

Objective: Follow directions and try recipe.

Objective: Have friends over to try something I have made.

****

The next page gives you an opportunity to develop some goals and objectives for yourself. Remember to make them realistic. It can be really frustrating setting up goals that are impossible to accomplish. It is usually best to start out with goals that are smaller and within your reach and work your way up to goals that are more complicated and time consuming. You may learn more about yourself from the process than you do from achieving the goal.

Goal: _____

Objective:

_____

_____

Objective:

_____

_____

Objective:

_____

_____

Objective:

_____

_____

Goal: _____

Objective:

_____

_____

Objective:

_____

_____

Objective:

_____

_____

Goal: _____

Objective:

_____

_____

Objective:

_____

_____

Objective:

_____

_____

Looking Back...Looking Forward

Think for a moment about the progress you have made in healing from the sexual abuse you experienced.

What steps did you take in this journey?

_____
_____
_____
_____
_____
_____
_____
_____
_____
_____

Think for a moment about the progress you would still like to make in your healing.

What additional steps do you need to take in this journey?

_____
_____
_____
_____
_____
_____
_____
_____

Wishes

Everybody has hopes and wishes. Having wishes sometimes helps people to set a direction and to develop a plan for themselves.

What are some of your wishes?
No wish is too far out for this exercise.

Moving Along
An art project for you

Make a collage that expresses your personality now or how you envision yourself in the future. It can express what you like, things you like to do, and things that describe the kind of person you are. Cut out pictures from magazines, color, draw, paint, or write words that describe yourself.

Supplies needed: paper, scissors, glue, magazines, crayons, pen, paints, or pencil.

Art Gallery

Draw a picture of yourself or place a photograph of yourself in the art gallery.

Self portrait of:_____ (artist)

Be sure to sign your portrait.

Measuring Scale:

Take a moment to complete this final measuring scale and appreciate the changes you have made.

Circle one:

I feel scared.	Always	Most of the time	Sometimes	Never
I like myself.	Always	Most of the time	Sometimes	Never
I feel sad.	Always	Most of the time	Sometimes	Never
I'm afraid.	Always	Most of the time	Sometimes	Never
I'm embarrassed.	Always	Most of the time	Sometimes	Never
I feel angry.	Always	Most of the time	Sometimes	Never
I'm happy.	Always	Most of the time	Sometimes	Never
I get upset.	Always	Most of the time	Sometimes	Never
I have nightmares.	Always	Most of the time	Sometimes	Never
I am a good person.	Always	Most of the time	Sometimes	Never
I'm shy.	Always	Most of the time	Sometimes	Never
I have friends.	Always	Most of the time	Sometimes	Never
I like other teens.	Always	Most of the time	Sometimes	Never
My family likes me.	Always	Most of the time	Sometimes	Never
I would be a good friend to have.	Always	Most of the time	Sometimes	Never
I'm excited about growing up.	Always	Most of the time	Sometimes	Never
I like my body.	Always	Most of the time	Sometimes	Never

I worry about how well other teens like me.	Always	Most of the time	Sometimes	Never
I feel attractive.	Always	Most of the time	Sometimes	Never
I feel fat.	Always	Most of the time	Sometimes	Never
I worry about having a boyfriend/girlfriend.	Always	Most of the time	Sometimes	Never
My friends like me.	Always	Most of the time	Sometimes	Never
I feel guilty when I eat.	Always	Most of the time	Sometimes	Never
I'm intelligent.	Always	Most of the time	Sometimes	Never
I'm creative.	Always	Most of the time	Sometimes	Never
I have a good sense of humor.	Always	Most of the time	Sometimes	Never
I am overly sensitive.	Always	Most of the time	Sometimes	Never
I cry.	Always	Most of the time	Sometimes	Never
I am self-conscious.	Always	Most of the time	Sometimes	Never
Other people think highly of me.	Always	Most of the time	Sometimes	Never
I get bored.	Always	Most of the time	Sometimes	Never
I prefer being alone to being with others.	Always	Most of the time	Sometimes	Never
I'm preoccupied with negative thoughts about myself.	Always	Most of the time	Sometimes	Never
I think about hurting myself.	Always	Most of the time	Sometimes	Never
I'd like to have more friends.	Always	Most of the time	Sometimes	Never
Adults care about me.	Always	Most of the time	Sometimes	Never

Messages To Remember

I am special.

I am loved.

I don't have to try to be perfect. I'm great just the way I am.

I am healthy.

I like myself.

I am a good friend.

I can succeed.

People like me and care about me.

I am a special and unique person.

I feel good about myself.

I accept myself just the way I am.

I trust my intuition.

I like being me.

Dear Teen,

Congratulations! You have reached the end of the exercises in this book. We hope this book has been helpful to you. It is our hope that you realize what a special and unique person you truly are. We wish you all the best in the future!

Yours Truly,

Phyllis & Randi

P.S. We will be writing a book with letters and pictures that teens have sent to us. If you would like to write to us about your experiences or send any material to us, we would love to hear from you. Please let us know if you would like your materials to be included in our book. We will not use your material without first getting your permission and your parent's permission. We hope to hear from you!

Please address your letters to: Phyllis and Randi

C/O Jalice Publishers

P.O. Box 455

Notre Dame, IN 46556

Special phone list of supportive people in my life:

Name   Phone number

1. _____   _____

2. _____   _____

3. _____   _____

4. _____   _____

5. _____   _____

Recommended Readings

Sexual Abuse

Daugherty, L.B. (1984). *Why me? Help for victims of child sexual abuse.* Racine, WI: Mother Courage Press.

Drake, E., & Gilroy Nelson, A. (1983). *Getting it together: Helping you to help yourself.* Gainesville, FL: Childcare Publications.
(for females who have been abused)

Drake, E., Gilroy Nelson, A. & Roane, T. (1983). *Working together: A team effort.* Gainesville, FL: Childcare Publications.
(for males who have been abused)

Gil, E. (1984). *Outgrowing the pain: A book for and about adults abused as children.* Rockville, MD: Launch Press.

Lew, M. (1988). *Victims no longer: Men recovering from incest and other sexual child abuse.* New York, NY: Harper & Row Publishers.
(for males who have been abused)

Taylor, M. (1990). *For guys my age: A book about sexual abuse for young men.* Whitmore Lake, MI: Hawthorn Center Clinic.
(for males who have been abused.)

Your Body and Sexuality

Bell, R. (1981). *Changing bodies, changing lives.* New York, NY: Vintage Books.

Gordon, S. (1975). *The teenage survival book.* New York, NY: Random House Publishing.

Powell, E. (1991). *Talking back to sexual pressure: What to say.* Minneapolis, MN: CompCare Publishers.

Certificate of Accomplishment

This is to acknowledge that

_____

has completed work in **High Tops.**

Congratulations!

Therapist: _____

_____

Date:_____

OUTSTANDING ACCOMPLISHMENT SEAL OF